CORNERSTONES OF FREEDOM™

THE LOUISIANA PURCHASE

BY PETER BENOIT

CHILDREN'S PRESS®

An Imprint of Scholastic Inc.
New York   Toronto   London   Auckland   Sydney
Mexico City   New Delhi   Hong Kong
Danbury, Connecticut

BRINGING HISTORY to LIFE

Content Consultant
James Marten, PhD
Professor and Chair, History Department
Marquette University
Milwaukee, Wisconsin

Library of Congress Cataloging-in-Publication Data
Benoit, Peter, 1955–
  The Louisiana Purchase/by Peter Benoit.
    p. cm.—(Cornerstones of freedom)
  Includes bibliographical references and index.
  ISBN-13: 978-0-531-23060-2 (lib. bdg.)   ISBN-10: 0-531-23060-0 (lib. bdg.)
  ISBN-13: 978-0-531-28160-4 (pbk.)   ISBN-10: 0-531-28160-4 (pbk.)
  1. Louisiana Purchase—Juvenile literature. I. Title.
  E333.B46 2012
  973.4'6—dc23   2011031342

1 2 3 4 5 6 7 8 9 10 R 21 20 19 18 17 16 15 14 13 12

Photographs © 2012: Alamy Images/North Wind Picture Archives: 45;
American Antiquarian Society/James Akin: 37; AP Images/North Wind
Picture Archives: back cover, 10, 14, 22, 27, 36, 38; Bridgeman Art Library:
26 (Bibliotheque Nationale, Paris, France/Archives Charmet), 44 (Brooklyn
Museum of Art), 18 (Christie's Images), 20 (Fondation Dosne-Thiers/
musee Frederic Masson/Giraudon), 17 (Minnesota Historical Society),
43 (Oscar Beringhaus); Corbis Images: cover (Alfred Russell/Bettmann),
42 (J.L. Kraemer/Blue Lantern Studio); Getty Images: 8 (AB Hall of New
York), 47 (Dorling Kindersley), 15 (Hulton Archive); Library of Congress/
James Akin: 39; Michael Haynes-www.mhaynesart.com: 51; National
Archives and Records Administration: 33; North Wind Picture Archives:
57 top (Maryann Groves), 55 (Nancy Carter), 4 top, 5 top, 6, 7, 12, 24, 25,
48, 54, 58; Shutterstock, Inc./Alex Staroseltsev: 5 bottom, 46; Superstock,
Inc.: 35 (Alonzo Chappel/Visual & Written), 40 (David David Gallery), 23, 56
(Rembrandt Peale); The Granger Collection: 49 (N.C.Wyeth), 32 (Thor de
Thulstrup), 2, 3, 4 bottom, 16, 21, 28, 50, 57 bottom, 59; The Image Works/
Louis Dodd/akg-images: 30.

Maps by XNR Productions, Inc.

Did you know that studying history can be fun?

BRING HISTORY TO LIFE by becoming a history investigator. Examine the evidence (primary and secondary source materials); cross-examine the people and witnesses. Take a look at what was happening at the time—but be careful! What happened years ago might suddenly become incredibly interesting and change the way you think!

Contents

4

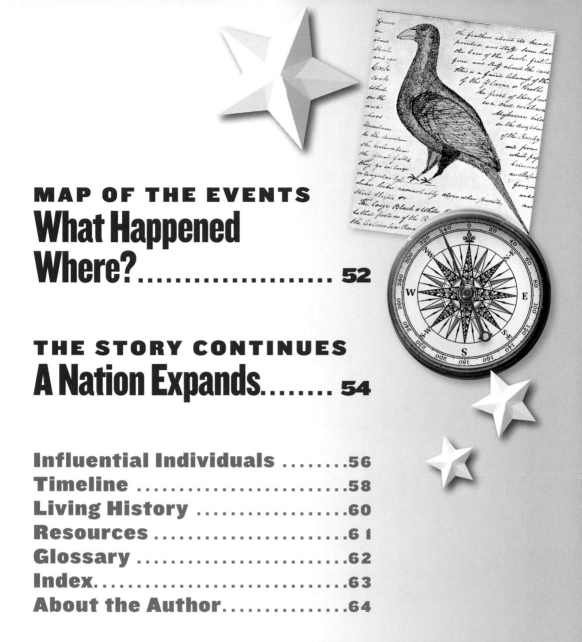

The Age of Discovery

European colonists quickly established settlements in the eastern portion of North America.

The United States was born in an age of discovery. Explorers from France, England, and Spain had charted portions of interior North America. Each country established colonies on the continent. Yet they rarely traveled west of the Appalachian Mountains. This part of the continent was thought of as a place of danger and possibilities. Few Europeans had seen it. But change was in the air.

Small bands of settlers had already begun to travel west by the time the United States was created. They built forts, houses, and villages in the Allegheny Mountains and Ohio River valley. But the Appalachians blocked trade with the eastern colonies. Settlers looked west to the Mississippi River as a trade route to the ocean, which could carry products to the eastern colonies and even Europe. The port city of New Orleans was located at the point where the river met the Gulf of Mexico. It soon became a desirable location. It had once been a French settlement but was now controlled by Spain. France, Great Britain, Spain, and the United States all knew that Louisiana would play a role in the future development of North America. Whoever controlled it could control the area's natural resources and trade along the Mississippi.

The Mississippi River was the most important waterway in North America.

AMERICA WAS ESTABLISHED IN 1607.

CHAPTER 1

GROWING PAINS

Even in the earliest days of the United States, Thomas Jefferson was greatly interested in exploring more of North America.

IN 1783, THOMAS JEFFERSON was Virginia's newly appointed representative to Congress. He had recently learned that a group in London wished to explore the interior of North America. Jefferson was alarmed. The American Revolution had drawn to a close in 1781. But the British continued to maintain forts around the Great Lakes. Their merchants and fur traders still sailed American rivers. Jefferson suspected that the London group was planning to expand Britain's interests in North America or perhaps even establish a new colony.

George Rogers Clark was best known as a hero of the Revolutionary War.

Jefferson's Idea

Jefferson suggested that the United States respond with its own **expedition**. He asked General George Rogers Clark to lead the expedition. Clark was a Kentucky **militia** leader whose Revolutionary War exploits had helped secure an American victory. Clark declined Jefferson's offer.

The planned British expedition also fell apart. But the idea of exploring farther west into North America lived on in Jefferson's mind.

Jefferson's concern over the proposed British expedition was well founded. Spain held a vast North American empire. It included Florida, the southern portions of Mississippi and Alabama, Mexico, and the wilderness south of Canada and west of the Mississippi River. But Spain's power was weakening. Its military had been in decline for more than a century. Jefferson knew that the death of

Spain's king Carlos III could result in a struggle for control of the great expanse to the west. He feared the French as much as he did the British. France's bases in the Caribbean could allow them to easily dispatch a military force. Many French people regretted the loss of Louisiana to Spain after the French and Indian War. They dreamed of regaining the territory.

Spain recognized the importance of Louisiana and the Mississippi. Louisiana served a defensive purpose. It kept foreigners a safe distance away from Mexico's silver mines. Half of the Spanish empire's **revenues** came from these mines. Defending Louisiana and New Orleans was very expensive, but Spain had little choice. The stability of its economy and government depended on Mexican silver.

Jefferson believed that the young United States was not prepared to fight for control of Louisiana if Spain lost its hold on the territory. The United States lacked the power to win such a struggle. But he also believed that the country's future depended on westward expansion.

A FIRSTHAND LOOK AT
JEFFERSON'S LETTER TO GEORGE ROGERS CLARK

Thomas Jefferson's December 4, 1783, letter to George Rogers Clark is filled with a sense of urgency. The Treaty of Paris had officially ended the Revolutionary War only three months earlier. Jefferson believed that it was important for the young nation to protect its interests. See page 60 for a link to read the letter online.

Early Westward Movement

Westward expansion was very difficult, especially for the first settlers who attempted it. The Appalachian Mountains were a geographic barrier to frontier farmers wishing to trade with coastal cities. Local rivers flowed south and west toward the Mississippi, which was controlled by Spain. Farmers couldn't use New Orleans as a point of export.

The interests of coastal merchants and frontiersmen had grown so different that talk about creating a separate nation had gained support in the Ohio River valley. Farmers argued that Congress did not represent their interests.

Many settlers began moving westward soon after the Revolutionary War.

King Carlos III sent **envoy** Don Diego de Gardoqui to New York to ease the growing tensions between the United States and Spanish Louisiana. Gardoqui arrived in spring 1785. He attempted to work toward a compromise with Secretary of Foreign Affairs John Jay. This effort was doomed from the start. The wealth of Spain's empire was at stake. Spain refused to listen to American requests to open the Mississippi. Gardoqui suggested that the matter be laid to rest for 25 years. He instead proposed giving the United States trading rights in Spain's ports in Europe and the Philippines.

A VIEW FROM ABROAD

Before the American Revolution, Great Britain viewed the westward expansion of its colonies with alarm. Native American attacks became more likely as the colonists pushed farther into the west. British leaders saw the matter as a threat to security. They passed the Proclamation of 1763 to discourage colonists from crossing the Appalachians. But about 30,000 farmers had moved west by 1773. Wealthy investors formed companies with the intent of selling land west of the Appalachians to farmers. In the end, the British did little to enforce the proclamation. Their military forces in America did not have enough firepower to press the issue.

This compromise satisfied New England, but it served to further anger the frontier farmers. Congress met to discuss the treaty that had been agreed upon by Jay and Gardoqui. In a speech before Congress, Charles Pinckney of South Carolina explained the farmers' arguments against the treaty in detail. He stated that Americans would pay higher tariffs in Spanish ports than the Spanish would pay in the United States. He also noted that no offer had been made for trade in Spain's Caribbean ports. Pinckney rightly pointed out that the compromise did not offer the United States any privileges it did not already hold. He claimed that it was merely a way for Spain to avoid the question of U.S. rights to use the

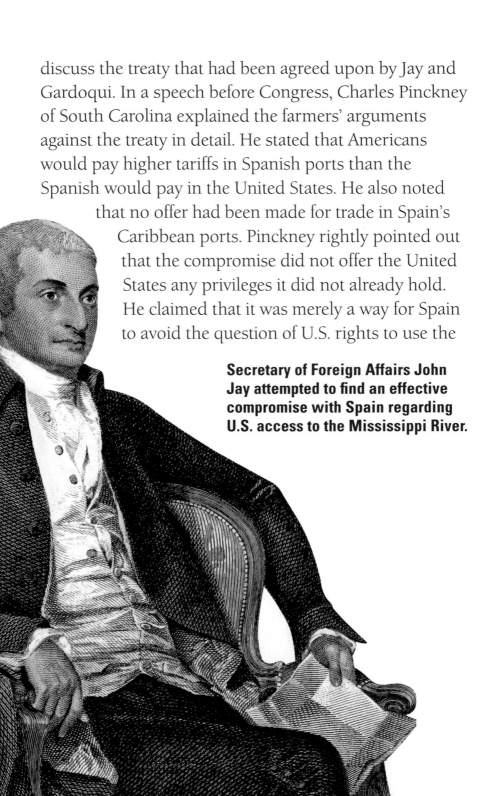

Secretary of Foreign Affairs John Jay attempted to find an effective compromise with Spain regarding U.S. access to the Mississippi River.

Mississippi River and the New Orleans port. Pinckney's arguments were persuasive. The treaty was never **ratified**.

The Treaty of San Lorenzo

Even though the treaty was dead, it continued to divide Congress. The unrest occasionally resulted in attacks against the Spaniards along the Mississippi. Spain finally signed the Treaty of San Lorenzo in 1795. It gave the United States the **right of deposit** in New Orleans. This allowed American merchants to store goods in Spanish New Orleans before they were shipped to other markets.

SPOTLIGHT ON

Charles Pinckney

Charles Pinckney was just shy of 29 years old when he argued against John Jay's treaty before Congress on August 16, 1786. His speech gave weight to the objections of the treaty's opponents and helped to stall it in Congress. It was only the beginning of Pinckney's rise in the U.S. government.

Pinckney was born in Charleston, South Carolina, in 1757. He became a lawyer in 1779 and entered politics soon after. He served as a member of the South Carolina legislature, a governor, a senator, and a representative during his career. Pinckney made important contributions to the U.S. Constitution when it was created in 1787.

Spain took away this right three years later. Frontier farmers were outraged. But their frustrations concerned

Gardoqui purposely increased tension between different parts of the United States.

New England merchants less. New England congressmen believed that preventing the frontier farmers from trading would discourage others from following them westward. Westward movement had weakened New England's power in Congress. It had also placed the farmers at odds with New England policies.

Gardoqui's diplomacy had caused conflict between different parts of the country. This weakened the Union. He had played to each group's interests to divide and conquer them. This made it more difficult than ever for these U.S. groups to reach an agreement. Gardoqui had believed that America posed a threat to Mexico's economy. Now this imagined threat was removed. But others in the Spanish empire saw a benefit to free trade and **immigration**. Louisiana's economic development could itself provide revenues to the Spanish crown.

Population growth upriver was much greater than that of New Orleans by the end of the 1700s. The population along the lower Mississippi might grow to match the north if restrictions on trade and immigration were lifted. Spain was stretched between the competing goals of lowering Louisiana's costs and protecting Mexico. It faced a conflict similar to that of the United States. Events abroad would soon give new life to Thomas Jefferson's vision of westward expansion.

In the 1700s and 1800s, many new settlements were established along the Mississippi River.

CHAPTER 2

FAVORED BY FORTUNE

Napoléon Bonaparte
believed strongly in
expanding France's
power around the world.

Frontier unrest at the end of the 1700s made Spanish officials wonder if it might be in their best interests to return Louisiana to French rule. The United States' westward expansion brought more and more traders into conflict with Louisiana's governors. The expense of maintaining Louisiana drained Spanish resources. France was more than willing to accept control of the territory. First Consul of France Napoléon Bonaparte finalized the Treaty of San Ildefonso with Spain on March 21, 1801. The treaty would return ownership of Louisiana to France.

Celebrations broke out in France as people learned of the Treaty of Amiens, which called for peace between France and Great Britain.

Louisiana's Uncertain Future

Nothing happened in Louisiana at first. The Treaty of San Ildefonso was unclear about one important point. Spain wanted a promise from France that it would not transfer Louisiana to a third party. France had offered a verbal promise. But oral contracts were not legally binding. Spanish chief minister Pedro Cevallos pressed for a written promise. Napoléon grew angry when negotiations stalled. A written agreement did not come until October 15, 1802.

In 1801, Louisiana's local government restored the right of deposit in New Orleans to American merchants and farmers. Great Britain had returned two eastern Caribbean outposts to France in the 1802 Treaty of Amiens. Since then, Napoléon had dreamed of a new empire founded on Caribbean sugar **plantations**. The colony of Saint-Domingue on Hispaniola had been established in 1659 and was already an important source of revenue. Napoléon saw Louisiana as a **depot** for his sugar empire. But this was only known by people inside the Spanish and French governments.

Jefferson became aware of Napoléon's plans in the Caribbean. He also knew that the right of deposit might be withdrawn again once Napoléon took possession of New Orleans. The arrangement was not set on solid ground and could collapse at any moment. The last time

The sugar plantations of Saint-Domingue were very profitable for the French empire.

Piracy and smuggling were common problems in New Orleans.

the right of deposit was taken away, a wave of smuggling and violence had occurred. Further expansion into the west and growing U.S. economic concerns continued to feed the violence even after the right of deposit had been restored. Louisiana administrator Juan Ventura Morales soon grew fed up with the smuggling and violence. He announced in October 1802 that he planned to take away the right of deposit once again.

A Peaceful Solution

Thomas Jefferson became president of the United States in 1801. That year, he authorized Robert Livingston, the U.S. minister to France, to seek a peaceful solution to the Louisiana problem. Jefferson had noticed the slow weakening of Spain's control over Louisiana. He felt certain that he could eventually win the territory piece by piece. He knew that opportunity would be lost with the return of Louisiana to France and Napoléon. The arrangement would place the United States permanently at odds with France. Jefferson authorized Livingston to try to purchase New Orleans and the surrounding area for up to $2 million.

TODAY'S PERSPECTIVE

Jefferson and Napoléon were both aware that the Louisiana Purchase would violate the terms of the Treaty of San Ildefonso. The deal would bring resistance from Jefferson's political rivals. New England **Federalists** were especially sure to oppose it. France was the only European power to recognize the purchase as valid. But Jefferson did not give in to the pressure from his political opponents. Control of New Orleans was necessary for the economic welfare of the United States. The Louisiana Purchase is still considered unconstitutional by many historians. But it is recognized as a practical solution to a difficult situation.

James Monroe went on to become the fifth president of the United States.

Morales's decision to remove the right of deposit added new urgency to Jefferson's message. Many Americans pressed for war with France. Jefferson hoped to avoid a bloody solution. He instead worked to convince the French that the costs of war would make possession of New Orleans a poor economic choice. He also sent envoy James Monroe to negotiate with Napoléon. The United States was now willing to offer up to $10 million for New Orleans.

The Haitian Revolution

The standoff between the United States and France was finally broken by events in Saint-Domingue. The colony's slaves had been in rebellion against the ruling white minority for about a decade. In 1792, the island's white population had refused to follow new French laws allowing for the citizenship of freed slaves. This encouraged the enslaved Africans on the island to revolt. In addition to a basic desire for freedom, they also had a fear that white colonials would rule more harshly now that the colonists were refusing to follow French law.

Haitian general Toussaint Louverture and his army of enslaved people succeeded in abolishing slavery in Saint-Domingue by 1794. Louverture overcame local rivals and installed himself as governor in 1801. He then declared full independence from France. Napoléon was greatly angered

YESTERDAY'S HEADLINES

Many U.S. slave owners liked the idea of slavery expanding into rich new territories. But they also feared the possibility of a slave revolt like the one that happened in Haiti. Jefferson did his best to distance the United States from Toussaint Louverture and the revolt. At the time, Edward Stevens was the U.S. diplomat to Saint-Domingue. Jefferson removed him and appointed Tobias Lear as diplomat. Louverture had built up trust and respect with Stevens. He considered the appointment of a new diplomat as a rejection of the revolution. Yet it was the French defeat during the revolution in Saint-Domingue that paved the way for the Louisiana Purchase.

by this situation. He sent an army of 40,000 soldiers to fight against Louverture's forces. A bloody war took place in Saint-Domingue over the next several months. The stubborn resistance of Louverture's forces combined with waves of yellow fever to force the French army out of the colony. The loss of Haiti's sugar plantations and growing anger against France in the United States led Napoléon to abandon his dream of a Caribbean empire. Louisiana no longer mattered to him. Saint-Domingue officially won its independence and was renamed Haiti in 1804.

Toussaint Louverture was widely respected and admired throughout Saint-Domingue.

Napoléon's New Plan

Napoléon turned his attention to Europe. He knew he might lose newly regained Louisiana to his rivals. There were 20 British warships in the Gulf of Mexico. Napoléon did not want to defend New Orleans against the British. He realized he would need money to wage war. He reasoned that selling Louisiana to the United States would remove the need to defend it. He directed his ministers to press for the sale of the entire Louisiana Territory. Napoléon ignored France's promise to Spain to never transfer the territory to a third party.

Napoléon made enemies throughout Europe in his quest to increase France's power.

On May 2, 1803, Livingston and Monroe signed the treaty that sold Louisiana to the United States.

This turn of events caught Livingston by surprise. The negotiators quickly agreed on the full sale of Louisiana. They now had to come to terms on a price. Napoléon's ministers suggested $25 million at first. Livingston knew that he would never win approval for such a large amount. Both parties sensed that the opportunity to strike a deal was slipping away. The negotiations grew more intense. Finally, they reached an agreement on April 30, 1803. France would sell Louisiana for about $15 million. A treaty was presented to Livingston and Monroe for approval on May 2. The signing of the treaty added nearly 830,000 square miles (2.1 million square kilometers) to the United States, doubling the country's land area.

News of the purchase reached the United States by the end of June. The *New York Evening Post* and Boston's *Independent Chronicle* reported it on June 30. Reactions to the purchase were mixed. General Horatio Gates called the purchase the "most beneficial event that has taken place since the Declaration of Independence." On the other hand, the *Balance, and Columbian Repository* questioned whether Jefferson had purchased "an immense wilderness for the purpose of cultivating it with the labor of slaves." The economic and political future of the United States had been bought in the remarkable land deal. But it would be a future troubled by questions with no easy answers.

A FIRSTHAND LOOK AT
THE LOUISIANA PURCHASE

The Louisiana Purchase eased the tensions that had developed between the United States and France. The United States doubled its land area for roughly $15 million. It also solved the economic and political issues raised by its westward expansion. See page 60 for a link to view the original document online.

CHAPTER 3

MIXED BLESSINGS

The Louisiana Purchase allowed American farmers and merchants to ship their goods up and down the length of the Mississippi River.

NEWS OF THE LOUISIANA

Purchase did not reach Jefferson until the evening of July 3. He knew nothing of the new land's boundaries or how much it had cost. Congratulations poured in even before the treaty was delivered on July 4. There were obvious benefits in controlling both banks of the Mississippi. The United States was now protected from Europe's wars and politics. Other people noted that taking control of Louisiana was an important step toward self-sufficiency. They believed that it might help to ease tensions between different parts of the country. The frontier farmers and merchants could finally pursue their interests without restriction.

The U.S. flag was raised in New Orleans on December 20, 1803, marking that Louisiana now belonged to the United States.

An Illegal Purchase

Napoléon insisted that the treaty be ratified by October 30. Congress gathered on October 17. It overwhelmingly approved the treaty and authorized Jefferson to take possession of Louisiana. Jefferson wished to avoid angering those people who lived in Louisiana and were used to Spanish rule. He appointed William Claiborne to act as governor. Claiborne was instructed to uphold the Spanish laws during the transition. France finally turned New Orleans over to the United States on December 20, 1803.

Jefferson's concerns about an orderly transition were well-founded. The Treaty of San Ildefonso had forbidden France to sell Louisiana to a third party. Jefferson and Napoléon had both known this. Napoléon also needed the approval of France's legislative assemblies to complete the transaction legally. He failed to get this approval. This made the Louisiana Purchase illegal according to French law. As a result, Great Britain and other European nations failed to recognize the legality of the transfer.

President Jefferson was concerned that the Louisiana Purchase violated the U.S. Constitution.

Article III of the treaty especially troubled Jefferson. It stated that anyone living in Louisiana became a U.S. citizen with the signing of the treaty.

Jefferson also had doubts about the sale's constitutionality in the United States. He had a reputation for supporting limited government and a strict interpretation of the Constitution. He wrote in a letter to Kentucky senator John Dickinson that the Constitution had not given the federal government "a power of holding foreign territory, and still less of incorporating it into the Union." Jefferson believed that a constitutional amendment was the only way to make the purchase legal.

But when Congress easily passed the purchase from France, Jefferson's amendment was deemed unnecessary. By passing it, Congress had already accepted the purchase as legal.

A FIRSTHAND LOOK AT
JEFFERSON'S DRAFT ON AN AMENDMENT TO THE CONSTITUTION

Jefferson himself believed that the Constitution did not permit the terms of the Louisiana Purchase. So he drafted an amendment to the Constitution that would make the purchase legal. The draft was never proposed to Congress. See page 60 for a link to read Jefferson's amendment draft online.

New Problems

The Louisiana Purchase caused an immediate increase in the size and racial diversity of the United States. This raised several concerns. Some doubted that so large an area could be effectively governed. The Union had nearly been torn apart by conflicts raised during the Jay-Gardoqui negotiations. Things would be worse when the area of the United

Federalist Fisher Ames was among the most vocal critics of the Louisiana Purchase.

States was doubled. Fisher Ames of Massachusetts was an influential Federalist. He imagined Louisiana to be "a wilderness unpeopled with any beings except wolves and wandering Indians." Ames felt that vast amounts of money had been wasted. He believed that the area east of the Mississippi River contained more than enough space for the country's people.

Ames and many others feared that Jefferson's decision would increase the popularity of slavery. They believed that any states created in the new territory

would share Virginia's economic and political concerns.
Because each would have two Senate votes, control of the
Senate would be lost for all time to slave-owning states.
The Louisiana Purchase brought the Federalists' concern
with race into focus.

Ames characterized the French, Spanish, and German
people of New Orleans as the unwanted waste of
Europe. Josiah Quincy III, a Federalist who would serve

**Many Americans
feared that slavery
would soon spread
into the new territory.**

as president of Harvard University from 1829 to 1845, called them "thick-skinned beasts." The Louisiana Purchase had increased tensions between the different parts of the country. The new territory threatened to tear the nation apart.

Napoléon grew impatient as Jefferson struggled with angry New England Federalists and the constitutional issues of the deal. He demanded that the United States secure the money to pay for the purchase. Napoléon had already threatened to break the treaty if Congress failed to ratify it. Now he suggested that he would break it if payment were delayed. James Monroe began working with banks in London and Amsterdam to finance the purchase.

YESTERDAY'S HEADLINES

Philadelphia cartoonist James Akin used rumors of Jefferson's relationship with an enslaved woman named Sally Hemings to comment on the relationship between slavery and the United States. In Akin's cartoon, Jefferson is drawn as a rooster and Hemings is drawn as a hen. The cartoon suggests that presidential power and national identity in the United States were closely linked with slavery. Many people believed that the president depended on slavery even though he would not admit it.

Maps drawn shortly after the Louisiana Purchase showed only the mapmakers' best guess about the size and shape of the Louisiana Purchase. No one knew its exact size.

Jefferson was at the center of a major controversy. He had drawn the suspicions of Federalists when he took office in 1801. Presidents Washington and Adams had enlarged the powers of the federal government at the expense of states' rights. Jefferson had promised to reduce that power. But now he did exactly the opposite by authorizing the Louisiana Purchase. The Federalists mocked him for going back on his promise.

The United States had gone into debt to purchase a wilderness that many people imagined to be swampland. Its boundaries were poorly defined. The Mississippi River was accepted as the eastern boundary. There was less agreement about northern and southern ones. Exact boundaries would not be set for another 15 years.

Even before the Louisiana Purchase was finalized, Jefferson had begun careful preparations for exploring and mapping it. This would help to create a western boundary. Jefferson's vision of westward exploration was finally about to be realized. This vision would take a shape that no one could have imagined.

YESTERDAY'S HEADLINES

In 1805, Jefferson planned to further enlarge the Louisiana Purchase. He began negotiating to purchase West Florida from Spain. Many people were critical of Jefferson's plans. Cartoonist James Akin once again mocked him. This time, he drew Jefferson as a large dog vomiting gold coins. The illustration implied that the purchase would be a waste of money that the country could not afford. But Jefferson's deal for West Florida did not go through. The United States eventually won the territory in the War of 1812. It also took control of East Florida as a result of the Transcontinental Treaty of 1819.

CHAPTER 4

CORPS of DISCOVERY

Lewis and Clark finally fulfilled Jefferson's wish to explore farther west into the continent.

JEFFERSON HAD STARTED

planning a scientific expedition to the west even before he became president. It would go up the Missouri River, over the Rocky Mountains, and on to the Pacific Ocean. Jefferson had pressed for such an expedition in 1792 as vice president of the American Philosophical Society. It never occurred. But young army officer Meriwether Lewis had expressed interest in the project. After Jefferson was elected president, he hired Lewis as his aide. Jefferson chose Lewis to lead the expedition when it came time to explore the Louisiana Purchase. Lewis chose William Clark, the younger brother of George Rogers Clark, to help him.

Lewis and Clark kept careful records of the plants and animals they discovered on their journey.

Planning the Expedition

Planning the excursion west began in 1803 as Livingston and Monroe traveled to Paris to complete the purchase. Jefferson sent a letter to Congress on January 18 detailing his reasons for the expedition. He asked for $2,500. Congress approved Jefferson's plan and granted him the money he requested.

Jefferson told Lewis and Clark the full plan of the expedition. They were to do all he had promised Congress. But Jefferson also asked them to carefully record the territory's plant and animal life. They were to collect specimens whenever possible. They were to keep records of native tribes encountered and to form alliances with them when they could.

The explorers would eventually encounter around six dozen tribes during the expedition. Lewis and Clark were sometimes adopted into tribes through pipe-smoking rituals. Smoking the pipe was a pledge to honor promises to relatives, protect them in war, and share wealth in times of peace. Lewis and Clark gave ceremonial peace medals to the natives as tokens of their respect. They also gave practical gifts such as kettles and corn mills.

Lewis and Clark met a wide variety of Native American groups as they traveled across North America.

Lewis and Clark presented peace medals to the natives they met on their journey. The medals were given as a sign of the explorers' respect for the natives. The front of the medal showed an image of Thomas Jefferson. The back showed two hands shaking in friendship. See page 60 for a link to view photos of the medals online.

Jefferson knew that Lewis would need more scientific knowledge for the trip than he possessed. Lewis went through three months of intensive training in the natural sciences to prepare for the journey. He was also trained by a doctor to treat the illnesses and injuries that members of the expedition were likely to suffer. Remarkably, only one member of the expedition died during the journey.

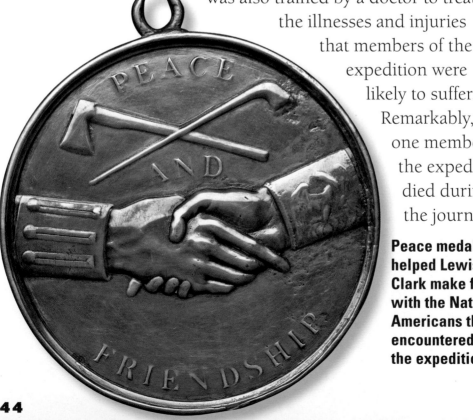

Peace medals helped Lewis and Clark make friends with the Native Americans they encountered on the expedition.

44

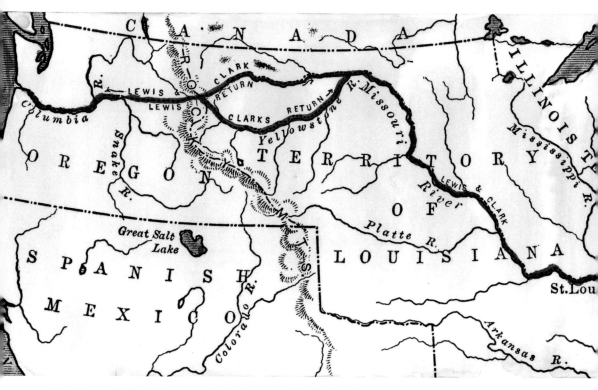

Lewis and Clark began their journey in St. Louis, Missouri.

The Journey Begins

Jefferson's "Corps of Discovery" consisted of about three dozen men when it set out from St. Louis, Missouri, on May 14, 1804. It included William Clark's slave, York, and a dog named Seaman. The men were prepared to collect data and create maps. They began the journey with a map compiled by War Department mapmaker Nicholas King. The King map reflected current understanding of the geography of Louisiana. It was created using earlier maps and reports. Information collected from fur traders was added to update the map. It helped guide the corps during its journey along

Equipping the Corps of Discovery

Two tons of goods were gathered to equip the expedition. They reflected both the practical concerns of a long wilderness journey and the scientific mission that lay at the center of Jefferson's plan. There were sophisticated instruments to aid in mapmaking and recording the weather. There were supplies to make camp life more bearable. There were also presents for native tribes, weapons for hunting, and medical supplies. Jefferson asked University of Pennsylvania physician Benjamin Rush to draw up a document with advice on how best to maintain the health of the Corps of Discovery. Lewis and Clark often ignored his advice in favor of the folk remedies recommended by natives.

the Missouri River. Lewis and Clark also produced about 140 of their own maps as they traveled. Measuring distance was important to making maps and discovering the size of the Louisiana Purchase. Jefferson equipped the Corps of Discovery with tools, including a compass and a telescope.

The Corps of Discovery kept careful logs of birds and other animals. They sometimes added sketches to their descriptions. In one entry, Clark commented on a sighting of the California condor. He thought that it might be "the largest bird of North America." The vivid entry is decorated with a sketch of the condor's distinctive shape. An 1805 entry details a meeting with a grizzly bear as the expedition broke from its winter camp at Fort Mandan and made its way toward the Milk River. Lewis gained a healthy respect for the creature when it chased him for 80 yards (73 meters).

The explorers discovered the pronghorn antelope, bighorn sheep, prairie dog, mule deer, mountain beaver, coyote, and mountain goat, among other species. They brought back claws, teeth, and skins. They also sent live creatures—a prairie dog, four magpies, and a sharp-tailed grouse—back to Washington. Lewis even returned east with a woodpecker specimen that survived the 28-month expedition. The corps discovered hundreds of species, including mammals, fish, birds, reptiles,

Grizzly bears were among the most dangerous animals Lewis and Clark encountered.

and plants. The Corps of Discovery collected several plant specimens. Some were important food sources. Others were common wildflowers.

Following the Rivers

The Lewis and Clark expedition had many scientific accomplishments. But it is best known for its record of the American wilderness. The men followed the Missouri River and found themselves in North Dakota in late October as winter began to set in. They chopped down cottonwoods that grew on the banks of the river and made a winter camp called Fort Mandan.

William Clark made detailed drawings, including this one, of many different plant and animal species.

The winter was unusually cold. The expedition did not break camp until the following April. The course of the expedition was changed in a remarkable way during that winter. French fur trader Toussaint Charbonneau and his young Shoshone wife, Sacagawea, joined the explorers. Sacagawea gave birth to Charbonneau's son on February 11, 1805. The whole family joined the Corps of Discovery when they left the camp on April 7.

Charbonneau added considerably to the expedition's understanding of the region's rivers, mountains, and native tribes. Sacagawea also proved invaluable. She

Sacagawea became a valuable member of the Corps of Discovery.

SPOTLIGHT ON

Sacagawea

Very little is known of the early life of this remarkable woman. Sacagawea was born into a Shoshone tribe in Idaho around 1786. The Hidatsa of North Dakota captured her in a raid in 1800. She was later sold to Toussaint Charbonneau, a French trapper. She and Charbonneau met Lewis and Clark at nearby Fort Mandan in the winter of 1804 to 1805. They joined the Corps of Discovery when it broke camp in April 1805. Sacagawea's role as an interpreter and peace delegate among native peoples was important to the expedition's success. She died December 20, 1812. Her short and extraordinary life is forever tied to the story of Lewis and Clark's journey.

acted as an interpreter and helped Lewis and Clark negotiate with the Shoshone. On May 14, 1805, one of the expedition's boats **capsized**. Many of the journals Lewis and Clark had so carefully kept fell into the river. Sacagawea saved the records. Much of what we know of the early expedition is owed to her fast response. Her greatest benefit lay in her mere presence. Because a woman traveled with the expedition, the natives understood its peaceful intentions. There were some tense encounters with the Lakota and Blackfeet, but warfare was less frequent than Lewis and Clark had expected. Peaceful relationships with **indigenous** tribes furthered the expedition's scientific goals.

The explorers pushed on to the mighty Missouri River. They climbed the rugged Bitterroot Mountains of the Idaho panhandle. They made their way along the Columbia River and finally reached the Oregon coast by early November 1805. They quickly built Fort Clatsop, and spent a miserable and lonely winter there. They waited for their opportunity to begin the return journey in the spring.

By the time they returned to St. Louis on September 23, 1806, more than two years after the start of their trip, Lewis and Clark had long since been given up for dead. But it was not death they had found in the wilderness. They found a land of great size and diversity. They discovered impressive wildlife and many native peoples. They had found the American West.

Because the expedition had taken so long, many people assumed that Lewis and Clark had died.

What Happened Where?

Lewis and Clark Expedition The long journey of Lewis and Clark and their Corps of Discovery helped to map out the western United States. Their incredible achievement led to the country's westward expansion.

New Orleans New Orleans was an important port city at the time of the Louisiana Purchase. It connected the Mississippi River to the Gulf of Mexico. Whoever controlled the city could control shipping up and down the river.

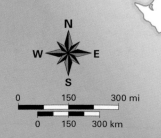

N
W   E
S

0   150   300 mi

0   150   300 km

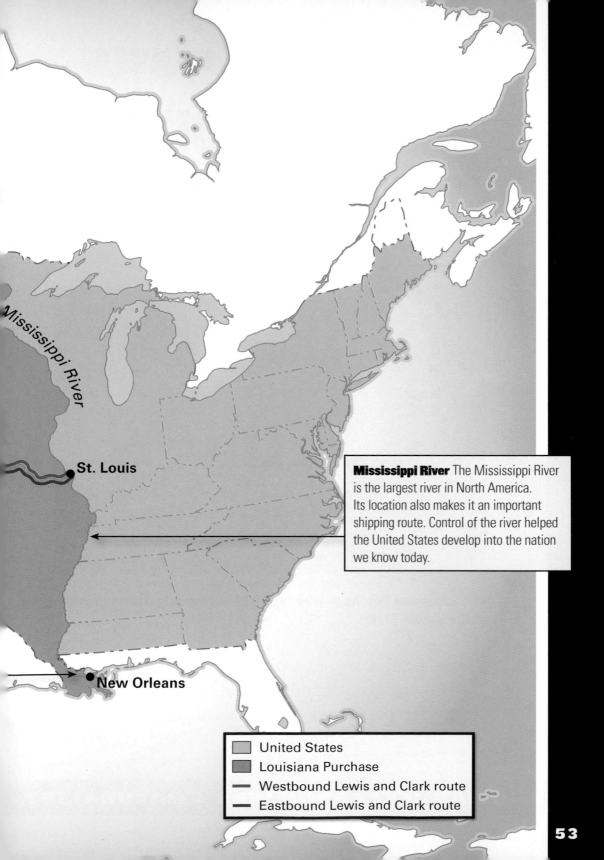

Mississippi River

St. Louis

Mississippi River The Mississippi River is the largest river in North America. Its location also makes it an important shipping route. Control of the river helped the United States develop into the nation we know today.

New Orleans

United States
Louisiana Purchase
— Westbound Lewis and Clark route
— Eastbound Lewis and Clark route

A Nation Expands

The Louisiana Purchase was the key to the westward expansion of the United States.

The fateful decision of adventurous colonists to cross the Appalachians set in motion a chain of events that would change America forever. Thousands of people were soon drawn westward by the promise of new land. The United

THOMAS JEFFERSON WAS A NATURALIST.

States began to develop into the country we know today. New settlements turned into towns and cities. New states were eventually added to the Union.

The Federalists were right to be concerned that the new territory would affect the debate on slavery. Debate over whether or not to allow slavery in the new states became one of the nation's greatest sources of conflict. Slave owners were outraged when the Missouri Compromise outlawed slavery in a large part of the new land in 1820. The Kansas-Nebraska Act of 1854 added to the debate by allowing the new territories of Kansas and Nebraska to decide for themselves whether or not to allow slavery. These conflicts would eventually become a major cause of the Civil War.

The Corps of Discovery has been honored with statues and monuments throughout the United States.

Thomas Jefferson

King Carlos III (1716–1788) was the king of Spain from 1759 to 1788. He used diplomacy to control the Mississippi River and protect his mining interests in Mexico.

Toussaint Louverture (1743–1803) was the leader of a successful slave revolt in the French colony of Saint-Domingue, now known as Haiti.

Thomas Jefferson (1743–1826) was the third president of the United States. He helped plan the Louisiana Purchase and the Lewis and Clark expedition.

Robert Livingston (1746–1813) was an American diplomat under Jefferson. He negotiated the purchase of Louisiana in 1803.

George Rogers Clark (1752–1818) was a heroic Revolutionary War general who declined Jefferson's offer to lead a western expedition in 1783. He was the older brother of William Clark.

James Monroe (1758–1831) was a U.S. ambassador under Jefferson. He helped to preserve the Louisiana Purchase by negotiating financing for the venture. He became the fifth president of the United States.

Napoléon Bonaparte (1769–1821) was first consul and later the emperor of France. He sold Louisiana to the United States in 1803 to raise money for war.

James Monroe

William Clark (1770–1838) was coleader of the Corps of Discovery and the younger brother of General George Rogers Clark.

Meriwether Lewis (1774–1809) was coleader of the Corps of Discovery and its main scientist.

Sacagawea (ca. 1786–1812) was a young Shoshone woman who joined the Corps of Discovery in the winter of 1804 to 1805 at Fort Mandan. She was an interpreter and occasional guide. She helped convince native tribes of the peaceful intentions of Lewis and Clark.

Sacagawea

TIMELINE

1783
George Rogers Clark declines a western expedition proposed by Jefferson.

1786
The Jay-Gardoqui Treaty is signed.

1795
Spain grants the United States the right of deposit in New Orleans.

1802
October
Permanent revocation of the U.S. right of deposit is threatened.

Jefferson sends James Monroe to France.

1803
April 30

The Louisiana Purchase Treaty is signed.

1798

Spain revokes the U.S. right of deposit in New Orleans.

1801

Thomas Jefferson becomes president of the United States; Jefferson sends diplomat Robert Livingston to France.

1804

January 1
Saint-Domingue wins independence from France and is renamed Haiti.

May 14
The Corps of Discovery leaves St. Louis.

1804–1805

Winter
Sacagawea joins the Corps of Discovery.

1806

September 23
The Corps of Discovery returns to St. Louis.

LIVING HISTORY

Primary sources provide firsthand evidence about a topic. Witnesses to a historical event create primary sources. They include autobiographies, newspaper reports of the time, oral histories, photographs, and memoirs. A secondary source analyzes primary sources, and is one step or more removed from the event. Secondary sources include textbooks, encyclopedias, and commentaries.

Jefferson's Draft on an Amendment to the Constitution

Thomas Jefferson believed that the only way to make the Louisiana Purchase constitutional was to amend the Constitution itself. You can read his draft for this potential amendment by visiting *http://avalon .law.yale.edu/19th_century/jeffdraf.asp*

Jefferson's Letter to George Rogers Clark
Thomas Jefferson's 1783 letter to George Rogers Clark shows that he was thinking of westward exploration even in the earliest days of the United States. You can read the text of the letter by visiting *http:// avalon.law.yale.edu/18th_century/let21.asp*

The Louisiana Purchase
The Louisiana Purchase more than doubled the size of the United States and paved the way for future westward expansion. You can view the original document online by visiting *www.loc.gov/rr/program/bib/ourdocs/Louisiana.html*

Peace Medals
Lewis and Clark presented many of the natives they met on their journey with peace medals as a sign of respect and friendship. You can see photographs of the front and back of a medal by visiting the following links:
www.loc.gov/exhibits/lewisandclark/images/ree0041p1s.jpg
www.loc.gov/exhibits/lewisandclark/images/ree0041p2s.jpg

RESOURCES

Books

Berne, Emma Carlson. *Sacagawea: Crossing the Continent with Lewis & Clark*. New York: Sterling, 2010.

Blumberg, Rhoda. *York's Adventures with Lewis and Clark: An African-American's Part in the Great Expedition*. New York: HarperCollins Publishers, 2004.

Fradin, Dennis B. *The Louisiana Purchase*. Tarrytown, NY: Marshall Cavendish Benchmark, 2010.

Web Sites

Library of Congress—Rivers, Edens, Empires: Lewis & Clark and the Revealing of America
www.loc.gov/exhibits/lewisandclark/lewisandclark.html
View maps, letters, artifacts, and more primary sources from the Lewis and Clark Expedition.

National Geographic—The Lewis and Clark Journey Log
www.nationalgeographic.com/lewisandclark/journey_intro.html
Follow the journey of the Corps of Discovery with maps, read the expedition's journal entries, and learn about the high points of each leg of the journey.

PBS—Lewis and Clark
www.pbs.org/lewisandclark/
View interactive trail maps, a timeline, equipment, journals, archives, and more.

Visit this Scholastic Web site for more information on the Louisiana Purchase:
www.factsfornow.scholastic.com

GLOSSARY

capsized (KAP-sized) turned over in the water

depot (DEE-poh) a storage center

envoy (AHN-voi) diplomatic representative

expedition (ek-spuh-DISH-uhn) a long trip made for a specific purpose, such as for exploration

Federalists (FED-ur-uhl-ists) members of a U.S. political party that supported a strong federal government

immigration (im-uh-GRAY-shuhn) coming from abroad to live in another country

indigenous (in-DIJ-uh-nuss) native

militia (muh-LISH-uh) a group of people who are trained to fight but who aren't professional soldiers

plantations (plan-TAY-shuhnz) large farms in a warm climate where crops such as cotton, tobacco, and coffee are grown

ratified (RAT-uh-fyed) agreed to or approved officially

revenues (REV-uh-nooz) the money that a government gets from taxes and other sources

right of deposit (RITE UHV di-PAH-zit) right to store goods while awaiting their export

INDEX

Page numbers in *italics* indicate illustrations.

ABOUT THE AUTHOR

Peter Benoit is a graduate of Skidmore College in Saratoga Springs, New York. His degree is in mathematics. He has been a tutor and educator for many years. Peter has written more than two dozen books for Children's Press. He has written about ecosystems, disasters, and Native Americans, among other topics. He is also the author of more than 2,000 poems.